# PROCRASTINATING PROCRASTINATION

*Proven Strategies to Crush Habits of Delay & Indecision for Life!*

**By**

**Sensei Paul David**

# Copyright Page

PROCRASTINATING PROCRASTINATION: Proven Strategies to Crush Habits of Delay & Indecision for Life. By Sensei Paul David, Copyright © 2020

All Rights Reserved.

ISBN# 978-1-7771913-4-4 (Electronic Book)

ISBN# 978-1-990106-05-7 (Paperback)

This book is not authorized for free distribution copying.

www.senseipublishing.com

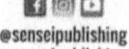

@senseipublishing
#senseipublishing

# Check Out Another Book In This Series Visit:

www.amazon.com/author/senseipauldavid

Or

Search Amazon.com #senseipublishing

# Get Our FREE Books Today!

## Click & Share The Links Below

## FREE Kids Books
lifeofbailey.senseipublishing.com
kidsonearth.senseipublishing.com

## FREE Self-Development Book For Every Family

senseiselfdevelopment.senseipublishing.com

# Join Our Publishing Journey!

If you would like to receive FUTURE FREE BOOKS and get to know us better, please click www.senseipublishing.com and join our newsletter by entering your email address in the pop-up box.

Follow/Like/Subscribe: Facebook, Instagram, YouTube: @senseipublishing

Scan the QR Code with your phone or tablet

to follow us on social media: Like / Subscribe / Follow

# Contents

**Foreward** .................................................................ix

**Chapter One Investigating the Origins of Procrastination** ......................................................1

Is Procrastination a product of nature or nurture? ...............................................................................1

Insights into Procrastination ...............................4

*Investigating how you Think* ..........................4

*Boredom* ...........................................................7

*Fear of Failure* ................................................7

*Fear of Expectations* ......................................8

*A Carefree Attitude* ........................................9

**Chapter Two Procrastinating Procrastination** 11

How to Procrastinate Procrastination ...............12

**Chapter Three The Triggers of Procrastination and Tips to Avoid the Response** ......................29

**Chapter Four  Reasons for your Lack of Motivation** ............................................................. 48

**Chapter Five  Flipping Procrastination to Action** ....................................................................... 63

**Chapter Six  The Final 20 Ways to Overcome Procrastination** .................................................... 75

**Index:** ......................................................................... 95

# Foreward

In the modern world, writing a book is no longer as challenging as it used to be. Therefore, many authors are putting out works by the day across the globe. Nonetheless, many so-called self-help materials out there do not offer value to the readers. Many only end up increasing the knowledge of the readers without adding practical steps that can give the readers a new lease of life. The good news is that this book is not one of such materials.

It is a practical guide based on the rich experience, astuteness, and expertise of the author. He is renowned for his uncanny ability to help people by simplifying seemingly complex concepts like chunking into short & easy to understand ideas. He is also adept at converting uncertainty into curiosity to form habits of continuous self-education. In 2002, he entered the corporate world and was introduced to having bigger responsibilities apart from his work.

That was when he started realizing that he needed to review his procrastination protocols. Before then, he was fond of doing things the hard way by starting with the biggest tasks. This approach led to frustration and delay in refocusing. He often struggled to take new actions because of the fear of failing. However, he was able to turn his life around. How? He realized that an early start leads to an early finish. He found out that a simple mental shift in notion could make a tremendous difference.

Things started getting better when he started taking massive actions with the maxim, "Early Start, Early finish." He started asking more questions, and he realized that he has been achieving improved results with almost anything he chooses to do. The idea of living life without delays started getting clearer, and he has drastically reduced wasting time when acting on an idea. He is more courageous to take action, believing that an early start will lead to an early finish.

Over the years, many people see him as the proponent of the adage "Early Start, Early Finish." Many individuals have also enjoyed success by adopting this maxim. Therefore, he has decided to come up with a comprehensive material that explains this procrastination-conquering mindset. This effort is what has given birth to this project. What do you stand to gain by reading this guide?

This book offers you a streamlined synopsis and solution strategies in one place. It also provides a path to action. This simple resource guide makes timely coaching available to you whenever you need it each step of the way and as often as you like. It is written in plain English with

FREE specialized bonus guided meditation. Therefore, you will be able to access a recap of the finer points of the book faster and easier than ever before.

# Thank You from The Author: Sensei Paul David

Before we dive in, I'd like to thank you for picking up this book. Your time is valuable, and I know there are many other similar books and courses out there that offer to help, but you chose to invest in mine, and that means everything to me.

Now that you're here, and if you stick with me, I promise to make our time together valuable and worthwhile.

In the pages ahead, you will find some areas of information and practices more helpful than others - and that's great because as you apply what works best for you. You will benefit from an exciting transformation of character and knowledge. Enjoy!

# Welcome

"Don't put off until tomorrow what you can do today."

*Benjamin Franklin*

Procrastination has always been a problem for many people, whether you work in an office or you perform your job at home. However, the COVID-19 pandemic has sent the world into a tailspin as many have started to work remotely to stay safe and slow the spread of the deadly virus.

Nowadays, it is even easier to start procrastinating because your mind is wandering, and you are focusing on other things. You get sidetracked.

**Let us explore ways to overcome your habits of delay and indecision.**

Congratulations on starting this and enjoy the process.

*Sensei Paul*

# Chapter One

## Investigating the Origins of Procrastination

**Is Procrastination a product of nature or nurture?**

This is an important question we need to answer. Indeed, procrastination is something we all do. However, some people seem to have more control over this habit than others. Could the answers be found in our genetic makeup? Placing the bulk of the fault at the feet of our parents is the easy way out for most of us.

We would claim that we are innocent because we are acting based on the training we received when we were younger. In some cases, we will look for any research out there that can prove that our bad habits are based on the way our brain was hardwired at an early age to perform the way we do as adults.

Interestingly, some studies have proven that procrastination can be traced to our genetic makeup. For example, the University of Colorado Boulder found in a study that procrastination is inherited. (1)

The above-mentioned study carried out by the University of Colorado Boulder also found the following:

- Procrastination is inheritable

- Impulsive actions and procrastination share a genetic variation
- Goal management is a part of procrastination and impulsivity

The study showed that 46 to 49 percent of people inherit procrastination and impulsivity. Therefore, genetics appears to influence how you effectively prioritize important goals and regulate your actions.

The good news is that whether you blame your procrastination on your genes, environment, or personality, it is fixable. Let us start to explore strategies and tips to help you overcome delaying things in your life and putting off until tomorrow what you should complete today.

## Insights into Procrastination

The best method to conquer procrastination is to first understand what it is and what it is not. Listing tips and strategies that can help against this bad habit might end up being useless if we don't understand the phenomenon we are up against.

### *Investigating how you Think*

In this section, we will perform a simple exercise that involves answering some questions that require honesty and sincerity. This concise test will help you to have an insight into how you think.

**Why do you procrastinate**? Could it be because you cannot carry out a task, or are you simply not interested in doing it? This question is simple, but it is foundational to stopping this limiting behaviour. Once you answer it sincerely, you have solved half of the problem.

**Are you inadequately equipped to perform the task?** Naturally, you will avoid a task that you lack the skills required to perform.

For example, you will not want to go near a pool if you don't know how to swim. You will do all you can to avoid any situation that will warrant you to swim because you know that you cannot do it. In the same way, a child will procrastinate about doing homework that he does not know how to tackle. You might wrongly assume that he is lazy. However, it is better to find out if he knows how to solve the problem in the first place.

Note that it is not always the case that you procrastinate because you cannot accomplish a task. There are also situations where you delay carrying out activity because you don't feel like doing it. For example, if you choose to delay mowing the grass of your house because it is sunny, it is not about a lack of ability, but you are just deciding not to do it.

You need to be able to identify your motive for delaying a task. The first step you need to take to conquer procrastination is to be able to know when you are choosing to avoid a task because you don't possess the skills to do it and when you just lack the enthusiasm to get it done.

## Boredom

The world is full of exciting toys that can distract you from doing what you need to do. In some cases, you prefer to play games or see a movie rather than do something productive with your time. One of the reasons you do this is because you don't find that task interesting. If a task makes you <u>feel bored</u>, then you are going to avoid it.

## Fear of Failure

The fear of failure is one of the most common reasons people procrastinate. No one wants to do something without getting a positive outcome. Therefore, it is natural that you avoid a task when you feel you are not likely to succeed in it. Fear of failure emerges at a young age.

When kids are fearful of the mockery of their peers, they often resort to avoidance. For example, they might delay participation in a sports competition because they don't feel they can succeed. Unfortunately, this fear continues into adulthood for many people. So, you need to recognize your fears and learn to tackle them to stop procrastinating.

**Fear of Expectations**

It sounds weird, but the reality is that some people are also afraid of success. They have enjoyed so much success in their lives that they become a victim of the expectations that comes with their previous success. When you achieve a lot, people tend to forget that you are human. They put so much pressure on you to always succeed. If you are not careful, you will start avoiding some tasks because you don't want to ruin the reputation you have built before now.

Many people who were superstars when they were young have ended tragically because of unmanaged expectations. Some of them ended up being drug addicts because they could not cope with the pressure. So, just like the fear of failure, you also need to watch out for fear of success.

## *A Carefree Attitude*

A carefree and nonchalant attitude will lead to laziness. Meanwhile, when you are lazy, you will procrastinate a lot. Laziness will affect your relationship because it will make you lose the trust of your loved ones. For example, your spouse might hire a helping hand to carry out chores because you make excuses for not doing them.

So, the earlier you destroy this harmful habit, the better for you. No one will want to trust you to handle anything significant when they cannot trust you to give it your best. Your skills and expertise will not be able to save you if you are not hardworking. Many will soon discover that you are not worth their trust due to your laziness.

## Chapter Two

### Procrastinating Procrastination

A double negative can have a multiplier effect to produce something positive, and that can be the case when it comes to procrastination. We have discussed the reasons people procrastinate. So, you are ready to learn how you can start tackling this bad habit. Indeed, you can reduce the rate at which you delay what you need to do. From this section and beyond, you will be exposed to tips and strategies for overcoming procrastination. Take your time to read through each one and select the ones that work for you.

## How to Procrastinate Procrastination

You can counter the tendency to procrastinate in your life by leveraging the following tips:

**Plan for Tomorrow**

You must plan for the next day. You will waste time when you wake up in a day, and you don't have things you need to do already. Planning and analyzing will waste time and end up wasting part of your peak period. So, take five minutes every day to plan for the next day.

**Stick to the Plan**

You need to have a plan and stick with it, especially when things get tougher. Note that challenges are parts and parcels of life. So, don't be perturbed when things are not going your way. Successful people rarely procrastinate because they have a plan, and they will stick with it. Changing your plans will make you waste time devising new strategies for the new goals.

## Measure your Self-Esteem

It is better to be overconfident than have low self-esteem. When you are self-confident, you will approach every task with assurance, which cuts out procrastination. However, when you have low self-esteem, you will not be confident of succeeding in a task. As a result of that, you will not want to attempt. Even when you choose to carry out the activity, you will not put in your best because you are not sure that things will go your way.

## Avoid Distractions

One of the things that lead to procrastination is when you are not focused. It is easier to be caught up in the web of digital devices in today's tech-savvy world. Many people cannot stop looking at their phones while working or carrying out a task. Such people will end up spending more than usual to do what they need to do. In some cases, you will have to postpone a task because you have wasted too much time on frivolities.

## Learn Until the End

You should ensure that you keep learning. It is normally,l like an old dog learning a new trick when you engage yourself in a task that is not familiar. However, if you have the right attitude, you can learn how to do anything. Once you keep your focus to learn from the beginning to the end, you will reduce the tendency to procrastinate.

**Give yourself Incentives**

Psychologists have done a lot of work on how incentives increase behaviour while punishment reduces it. If you have ever trained a dog, you will notice that it will perform an act more frequently when you reward it for doing it. In the same way, you can train yourself to inculcate the right habits by rewarding your good behaviours. For example, promise to have a nice treat when you perform a task within a specified period. The incentive will help you to keep working hard towards the goal. Over time, you might not need to reward yourself again because of the feeling of accomplishment after achieving a feat, by itself, is enough motivation to avoid procrastination.

**Forgive Yourself**

Interestingly, it is often easier to forgive others than forgive yourself. Unfortunately, you will only get stuck in the same position when you refuse to release yourself from the past hurt. Research has proven that you will reduce the rate of procrastination when you practice self-forgiveness. This is since you will create a more positive outlook of yourself when you let go of past mistakes. (2)

## Be Accountable

You should have the discipline to focus on what you need to do and get it done. However, it can be challenging to supervise yourself. If you are finding it difficult to concentrate and do what you need to do on time, you should consider asking a loved one to check on you. You likely focus on what you need to do and achieve it when you have someone who will find out about your progress rate. Besides, there are online tools such as the Procrastinator, which can help you to be proactive and self-monitor your time.

## Act Fast

According to Benjamin Franklin, "Don't put off until tomorrow what you can do today." These words say a lot about acting quickly instead of wasting time. You need to act fast. What do you have to lose when you choose to start now? So, start now!

## Limit Distractions

It is almost impossible to avoid distractions in the modern world. We all want to avoid being left behind. Besides, you have juicy discussions on social media you want to read every day. Nonetheless, you must find a way to limit your distractions to achieve your targets personally and in other areas of your life.

## Conquer Negative Self-Talk

The voices in your head are louder than the ones around you. Your mind is an active processor that absorbs both positive and negative stimuli around you. So, you need to stay in charge to avoid letting your mind on the loose. When you leave your mind on "auto-pilot mode," it will groom destructive thoughts that can lead to procrastination.

Empower yourself by changing the thoughts in your mind from a compulsion to choices. For example, you should not think, "I have to do this," rather, think, "I want to do this." This paradigm shift can give you a new lease of life to help you avoid delaying what you need to do.

## Eat that Frog

Many people make the mistake of approaching their tasks by starting from simpler tasks. This approach can lead to not having enough energy, later on, to carry out the more challenging ones. So, it is always better to do the difficult tasks first during your peak period.

**Work at Peak Periods**

Your peak periods are the parts of the day when you are the most effective. It is the part of the day you can focus your energy on a job and accomplish it. Find out what works best for you and work during that time.

**Leverage Time Management Tools**

Indeed, the modern world is full of distractions. However, we also have many tools out there that can help you manage your time and increase your efficiency. Individuals and organizations take advantage of time management apps to boost their productivity, and you can do the same. Trello and Toggl are some of the most popular options out there.

**Know when to Take a Break**

Taking a break is not evil if you know how to do it at the right time. Taking a break does not always mean that you are lazy. It can boost your efficiency. When you rest a bit after working hard, it can help you to refresh and have enough energy to work harder again. You cannot achieve much when you feel jaded. You might end up procrastinating because you have lost the zeal and energy to keep working.

## Get Your Blood Pumping

Many companies are going digital. Indeed, it comes with many advantages, such as working in the comfort of your home. It is also cost-effective for both companies and employees. However, it is easy to start slouching in your office chair and feel sleepy. You can start struggling to complete tasks because you have been too static while sitting for several hours in front of your computer. So, you need to take a break once in a while to get your blood pumping again. A quick workout will do the magic.

## Work with a Deadline

Working with a deadline reduces the chances of procrastination. One of the reasons you waste time on a task is that you feel you have excess time to complete it. One study discovered that the ideal way to time yourself is by working for 52 minutes and then give yourself 18 minutes to relax. If you are wasting too much time, you need to start giving yourself the deadline for your tasks. Be accountable to a person to ensure that you stick with it. (3)

**Sectionalize your Work**

One of the techniques to avoid mental exhaustion and procrastination is to break your work into sections. This method is crucial when the task is going to take a lot of time. You likely avoid starting a task when it is going to be very demanding. So, you should break it up into smaller bits. This technique of increasing efficiency is called **chunking**. Of course, it is just a trick of the mind. Nonetheless, it is effective for accomplishing demanding tasks.

**Reinvigorate yourself with a Snack**

Taking a snack can become a distraction if you are not careful. However, it is one of the best ways you can recharge without feeling tired. An apple or a banana are great foods to refuel. (4)

**Work with a Friend**

Your friends can inspire you to achieve your goals and accomplish your dreams. If you have a friend that has similar tasks to achieve, you can work together to inspire one another to stay focused. However, you need to know when to quit if the person ends up distracting you.

**Take Advantage of Social Media**

Social media has many ills to it. However, we cannot deny that it has many benefits if you learn to use it to your advantage. Many people take advantage of social media platforms to share different things, including recipes, images, and videos. You can also take advantage of the platform to share your targets with your friends and loved ones. When you tell your friends and families about your goals, you will be under pressure to ensure that you achieve them. Note that this approach may not be the best if you have many strangers as your "friends" on a platform like Facebook.

## Avoid Looking for the 'Perfect Time'

Many people end up not doing what they need to do because they were waiting for the perfect time to do it. For example, you might want to wait until the weather is cooler to mow the yard. You might not have the same enthusiasm to do it by that time. Besides, you might have to attend to something crucial and urgent by then. So, once you are free to do something, do it immediately.

## Reduce your Stress Levels

Stress is inevitable. However, you must learn to cope with it and manage it effectively. When your stress levels are high, you will not have the desire to do what you need to do on time. Therefore, you need to work on reducing your stress levels as much as possible. There are many ways you can achieve this. For example, you can explore to help you focus your mind and improve your mood. Gratitude does not mean that you have things going your way. Instead, it is a deliberate choice to focus on the positive aspects of your life rather than the negative parts.

So far, we have discussed some strategies and tips that can help you against procrastination. Subsequently, in the next chapter, we will dig deeper to help you have a better understanding of this subject. We will explore what leads to procrastination with a more detailed approach.

Instant gratification is the order of the day. The issue with this mindset is that it will prevent you from enjoying better and more significant benefits. One of the reasons we procrastinate is that what you need to do immediately does not offer any benefit at the moment. We will explore this issue and other relevant ones in the next section.

# Chapter Three

## The Triggers of Procrastination and Tips to Avoid the Response

We need to understand what triggers procrastination to cut out this destructive habit. According to Tim Picryl, the author of *Solving the Procrastination Puzzle:* seven triggers make us want to delay what we ought to do at the moment. (5) They include:

- Boring
- Ambiguous
- Frustrating

- Unstructured
- Lacking in personal meaning
- Difficult
- Not intrinsically rewarding

Nonetheless, many activities are in these categories. To carry out such tasks, you will have to mentally rename them to a different label, among other solutions to ensure that you do what you need to do. The tips in this chapter will help you arrest the slide.

**Keep a Journal**

Amazingly, keeping a journal has many benefits, including the improvement of mental health. Therefore, it is not surprising that many people are leveraging this concept to improve their efficiency and avoid procrastination. When you are writing, your mind is involved. So, the process creates an emotional connection to the things you are writing, thereby giving you the motivation to act on them. This technique is particularly important to the goal-setting process. You can also use journaling to practice gratitude. It involves writing things that make you happy in your life in your journal. If you have this culture, you will have more reasons to keep going during tough times and will avoid wasting time.

**Emotional Connection**

You cannot carry out a task enthusiastically when you are not emotionally connected to it. So, you need something that can make you have positive feelings while doing the activity. There are many ways you can achieve this. If the task will fetch you some money, think about all the nice things you can do with the money once you complete the job. Besides, if it is something that will enhance your career, think about all the perks that come with it such as the paycheck and respect.

**Resist the Urge**

The statement that emotions are antithetical to logic could not have been more correct. Our emotions are part of what makes life beautiful. However, they can be serious drawbacks that can make you procrastinate. So, do not give in to your emotions that are telling you to procrastinate. Instead, let your logic take control. In order words, focus more on the reasons you should work rather than check your social media app. The natural urge is to do things that are not stressful. However, you have to choose to be logical rather than emotional.

**Redefine the Triggers**

It is not good enough to know the triggers. It is also vital that you redefine them when performing a task to overcome procrastination. You can use the template below to do yours.

Example:
- Difficult = Demanding
- Boring = Misunderstood
- Ambiguous = Needs to be solved

- Frustrating = Requires skills
- Unstructured = In Progress
- Lacking in personal meaning = Needing relevance
- Not intrinsically rewarding = Delayed significant reward

Renaming tasks in this format sounds simple. However, it has tremendous impacts. By seeing a difficult task as challenging, you will push yourself to get the needed resources to succeed at it. You will look forward to the sense of achievement you will get after completing the task. In the same way, treat a seemingly boring task as misunderstood. One of the reasons we feel an activity is not exciting is that we don't understand how to go about it. You can turn things around by asking questions from other people who are more adept at carrying out the task.

## Know Your Resistance Level

Your resistance level is your breaking point. Once you get to that point, you will not want to perform any task. For example, you might struggle if you spend an hour reading and you want to spend the next hour preparing a report. This struggle shows that you have reached your resistance level. Once you get to that point, you will start getting frustrated. Therefore, you need to take a break. You should consider breaking a demanding task into segments to avoid getting exhausted. For example, you can spend thirty minutes on a part and move to the next one after ten minutes break.

## Be in Charge

Many books and articles have been written on the power of the mind. Indeed, the mind is a powerful thing. The way you train it can make or mar you. Your mind can make you avoid some tasks if you allow it to control you. When you think about something, then it can become worse than it is in reality. Instead, you need to just force yourself to start, and you will probably be amazed to find out that it is truly not as bad as you envisioned. It might be somewhat easy once you begin to work on the project and stop procrastinating. Therefore, you need to be in charge of your thought to control your emotions.

**Start with the Intention to Finish**

When you don't have the plan to finish a task you have started, any point can be the end. Research has proven that you will not feel at ease when you are yet to complete a project. So, the trick is to start first to finish. When you are determined to finish the work, you are most likely going to start immediately and push until the end. (6) Even if you did not manage to complete the task, you would have done enough to complete the rest as soon as possible.

**Think about how much Money Procrastination will Cost you**

When you think of the fact that delaying a project will make you lose money, you will be under pressure to get the job done at once. One of the ways you can inspire yourself is to think about how much you will earn when you are done with the work. This approach is particularly effective when what you are procrastinating about has financial gains to it. This simple formula can make you treat your projects with more urgency to get them done on time.

**Impact relationships**

The last thing you want is to lose the trust and affection of your loved ones. Indeed, family and friends are supposed to overlook your imperfections and still love you and support you. Nonetheless, you need to make it easier for them to do so. No one will hand over trust to you. You have to earn it through your actions.

Your friends and families will avoid trusting you with responsibilities when you have a knack for wasting time and giving excuses. They will rather look for someone that will not disappoint them. Procrastination can also affect your relationship with your spouse. It can lead to arguments, especially when you are not repentant and penitent. So, consider the effects time-wasting can have on your relationships to encourage you to make amends.

**Envision Your Success**

Think about what you stand to gain when you complete a task and let it inspire you to avoid delays. Experts call this approach a form of reverse engineering. It involves standing on the podium first and working from there to get to where you are. Keeping your eyes on the prize is a fantastic motivation technique that can inspire you to avoid putting off whatever you need to do now.

**Lack of Purpose**

Naturally, you will not commit to an activity when it does not make sense to you. For example, you cannot enjoy a game when you don't know its essence. If you see football as just a stupid game where people are shooting a ball into goalposts, you will not participate in the sport. One of the reasons you procrastinate is that you cannot see any reason you should carry out a task.

If it is something new to you, endeavour to ask questions from the right people so that you can have more insights into why it should be done. Until you find a reason to carry out an activity, you can never be enthusiastic to do it. So, you need to do some soul-searching until you find a common ground. Many online and face-to-face programs can help you search for meaning in life. Leverage them to give yourself a boost and overcome procrastination.

**Sense of Impeccability**

Your background and previous experiences can make you a perfectionist. Perhaps, you were an

"A" student in school, and you will never accept anything less than that. Indeed, there is nothing wrong with having an excellent academic record. Generally, you should want to be the best in whatever you are doing. However, life does not always give you what you want or even deserve. So, you need to avoid an obsession with perfection. Failure to do so will make you waste time and lose opportunities to start small. You can't always have a perfect score. So, you need to learn to take the positives and keep pushing rather than waiting for perfect opportunities to act.

**Fear**

It is okay to be afraid once in a while. We all have reasons to fear. So, you should not feel like a weakling when you are scared. However, it is a problem when you allow your fear to crush your confidence, making you procrastinate. Sometimes, the reason you are afraid is due to your past failures. Nonetheless, you have to forge ahead. You should learn from your past failures rather than make them reasons you cannot try again. You can turn your life around if only you are willing to do so. If you notice that you are often anxious and fearful, you should talk to a counsellor to help you with therapy. Nonetheless, the most effective therapy is self-determination to try again after failing.

**Truth Avoidance**

Misinformation has a great impact on a person's psychology. The University of Michigan carried out a study to validate this claim. The result showed that misinformation influence how you think. Interestingly, you might not even realize it. In some cases, these wrong beliefs will form your worldview and make you do the wrong things. You might even be subconsciously avoiding the truth and procrastinating so that you can stay in your comfort zone. So, you will have to take deliberate steps to liberate your mind to absorb the truth. This form of procrastination sounds strange but it is real. For some people, it is a survival mechanism for avoiding difficult situations. At the height of it, you will have to see a counsellor before you can reverse the effects of this self-imposed delusion. (7)

## Avoiding Demanding Tasks

One of the reasons people procrastinate is the avoidance of tasks they deem challenging and demanding. Thinking about how difficult a task is can drain your energy and reduce your mental strength to cope with it. In some cases, you will keep wasting time because you don't want to start. However, in some situations, you will start with smaller tasks first. It is still a form of procrastination because you might be too tired and mentally exhausted to tackle the demanding task when you are done with the easier tasks. So, your best bet is to face your fears and do the difficult tasks first.

## Low Motivation

Motivation is the fuel that powers every activity. Motivation is linked to your energy levels. When you are fatigued, you will not want to do anything. You might need to rest and eat to be ready again. Nonetheless, physical strength does not mean that you will have the desire to get something done. If you are physically sick, talk to your doctor on time because that will affect the urgency with which you carry out a task. In the same way, if you are mentally exhausted, you need to act fast. If it is a recurrent issue, you should consider speaking to a mental health expert.

## Lack of Clarity

You cannot be at your best if you lack direction. It is when you know what to do that you will know the direction to direct your energy and other resources. So, you will delay doing something when you are not sure about what you need to do. Don't hesitate to ask questions when you find yourself in a situation where you are confused. Asking questions will help you to have better insights into the task, thereby making you start working rather than delay what to do next.

## Chapter Four

### Reasons for your Lack of Motivation

If you don't know the reason you are acting in a particular way, you cannot stop that habit. For example, if you have issues with your temper, you need to find out the sources of your irritation and frustration to turn a new leaf. In the same way, you need to be able to find out why you lack the desire to carry out a particular task to be inspired to do and complete it.

Note that you cannot succeed in any endeavour if you don't have the zeal and passion to go all out to get it done. So, you must diagnose your lack of passion and fix it as soon as possible. Some people start to lack motivation because of something that is going on in their current life. This section will help you to discover the likely reasons you are not inspired to do something and the tips to overcome them.

Major causes of lack of motivation include:

- Stress
- Fatigue
- Depression
- Other more pressing needs
- Lack of new ideas
- An emergency

- Surrounding yourself with negative vibes
- Previous failures
- Working in a discouraging environment
- Ambiguous goals
- Global issues like a pandemic or recession

According to a study carried out by Carnegie Melon University, a lack of motivation is why many people procrastinate. Nonetheless, if an individual can connect a task with goals and intersects, the individual will feel more energized to get the work done. (8) So, seeing completing a task as crucial to your satisfaction and fulfilment can go a long way in encouraging and inspiring you to start immediately.

Goal choice and self-confidence are the two key components of motivation, according to researchcarried out by the National Academies of Sciences, Engineering, and Medicine. (9)

Setting goals gives you the direction to focus your energy. However, you cannot succeed by setting goals alone. If you don't have self-efficacy, your objectives can never be accomplished. One of the reasons you lack self-confidence is that you don't have the skills required to achieve your target.

There are many ways you can overcome a lack of motivation. The tips below are some of the most popular that has proven to be effective:

## Work Environment

Your work environment is crucial to your productivity. If you are working in a place that is full of distractions, you are not likely to have an engagement with the work. Note that some distractions are "positive." For example, if you are working at home, your spouse or children may need your attention. This distraction is positive because you are also strengthening the bond of your relationship by giving your loved ones your attention. Nonetheless, it is still a form of distraction. So, it is better to be in a place where you will not have to be distracted even for the right reasons.

## Ambiguous Objectives

Don't just set goals for the sake of it. Ensure you know what you want and write it down without ambiguity. For example, don't write, "I want to be the best in my career." Rather, write, "I want to make the most sales among the sales rep of my company this year." Something like this is more specific and can lead to prompt action.

## Identify Your Stressors

One of the reasons you lack motivation is stress. We cannot do without stress. However, we must be able to cope with it effectively to avoid getting mentally and physically exhausted. It is easy to be emotionally drained in recent times due to the COVID-19 pandemic. The report has it that millions of people around the world have died due to sickness. Many people are worried about the virus affecting their loved ones. This situation can drive your anxiety levels very high. Nonetheless, you need to realize that your worry will not protect your loved ones.

Instead, it will only take its toll on your mental health. The best thing you can do for them is to enlighten them about the preventive measures of the virus. Don't let the situation weigh you down such that it is affecting your efficiency. If there are other reasons you are stressed and lack motivation, identify them and relieve the stress. Note that junk food or alcohol consumption should not be options for you. A workout routine and meditation are better options that can help you relieve stress without side effects.

## Depression

Depression is a problem facing millions of people across the globe. This mental health condition results from stress and other factors. The advent of social media exposes many people to stressful and mentally challenging situations. Social comparison has never been easier, which leads to discontentment and lack of happiness. Many celebrities post their expensive accessories and mansions on these platforms. So, some people feel that something is wrong with them because they don't possess what those superstars possess.

Besides, some individuals have been victims of cyberbullying where many people mock them because of their body shape or other things. When you allow depression to get the best of you, you will not be motivated to work. Pay attention to the source of your depression. If it is due to your exposure to social media, you need to reduce the time you spend on those platforms. If you are still struggling to cope with depression after trying your best efforts to overcome it, see a counsellor as soon as possible.

**Tiredness**

Fatigue can be due to mental or physical exertion. Nonetheless, it is difficult to separate one from the other. If you are mentally exhausted, it will affect your motivation to do something. In the same way, you cannot be at your best when you are physically tired. Tiredness might mean that you are doing too much and need to slow down. If you discover that you are working too hard, you need to take a breather. You don't have to wait until you break down before you do the needful.

**Priorities**

When you fail to pay more attention to the things that matter to you the most, you will regret it eventually. When you are giving more time to the less relevant tasks, you will eventually lack the motivation to tackle the more crucial ones. Therefore, you must decide what your priority is and give it more time and attention.

## A dearth of Fresh Ideas

When you are finding it hard to come up with new ideas, it can lead to procrastination. Writers and researchers often face this challenge. In some cases, you are just staring at your laptop screen for minutes, waiting in vain for the next idea. One of the reasons you have this mental block is that you are not working during your peak periods. If that is the case, ensure that you find out the time of the day you are at the optimum level of energy to get the job done. Also, you can reach out to friends and family to pull in fresh ideas so that you again feel inspired.

## Unprecedented Events

Emergencies happen, and they can slow you down. Life is full of unprecedented situations that can ruin your plan. So, it is always good that you have another plan in case the first one does not materialize as expected. Some situations can be so shocking that they can make you lose focus and steal away all your energy or desire. However, your strength is revealed by how you react when you have to deal with an unexpected situation. Try to clear things up, accepting the fact that sometimes, things fall apart. When they do, we pick ourselves back up and refocus to get back on track.

## Previous Mistakes

Your past can either mar you or make you. It all depends on you. Many people have recovered from devastating situations to get their lives on track again. Such people become a source of inspiration for other people going through tough times today. In the same way, there have been people who have had setbacks and never recovered again. No one wants to repeat their past failures. The fear of falling short is enough to make anyone drag their feet. However, you cannot let fear stand in your way. You must forge ahead to try to overcome your past shortcomings. Let your mistakes serve as lessons that will act as springboards for your future success. You can choose to give up or keep fighting. However, the latter is always the better choice.

**Negative Vibes**

You cannot rule out the influences of the people around you on your life. The people around you can make you lose interest in the tasks you need to do or make you delay them. Some people will tell you that you are working too hard by being focused and committed. Some honest people can say that to you to protect you from breaking down. However, some people say things like this to you so that you will not make them look lazy. Stay around the people that will encourage you to be focused and committed to what you need to do.

## Chapter Five

## Flipping Procrastination to Action

It takes being watchful and guidance to make children do things that do not offer them immediate gratification. They prefer playing to doing tasks such as their assignment. As we grow older, we often retain this same mindset. We still prefer to watch our favourite TV show rather than do our laundry. We know that washing our clothes will make us look tidy and clean and prevent diseases in the long run. However, watching the TV show will make us excited immediately, and the natural tendency is to choose it.

Whenever you have to do tasks with the following features, you are likely to procrastinate:

- Difficult: We all prefer to avoid tasks that are demanding and time-consuming.
- Boring: No one wants to be involved in an activity that is not exciting.
- Unstructured: It is tricky to focus on when a project is not systematic and procedural.
- Frustrating: When you are not making progress while learning a new skill, you can get frustrated.

- No Intrinsic Rewards: A task that does not offer positive feedback will not feel interesting to you.
- Ambiguous: When a task does not seem to be leading to a specific destination, it leads to procrastination.
- Meaningless: If you cannot decipher the essence of carrying out a task, you will not want to commit to it.

Any task that has more of the above attributes will lead to delays. You will not find enough motivation to get it done immediately.

The tips below will enable you to flip tasks that have these attributes to your advantage:

**Make it Fun**

There are many creative ways you can bring more life into a task that drains you physically and mentally. One of them is by buying an audiobook that you can listen to while you perform mundane chores. Find out what works for you and incorporate it into your activities. Note that you can have a collection of methods for making a chore fun. Use them randomly to avoid getting bored.

**Set Aside Time**

Setting a deadline often inspires prompt action, which is critical to success in every sphere of life. When you set aside time to complete a task, you will restrict yourself from losing focus. It brings a sense of urgency to what you are doing, which helps you to overcome procrastination.

**Relax your Mind and Body**

Your body is like a machine. Therefore, you should not be surprised that it will start malfunctioning when you abuse it. One of the ways you can avoid overusing your body is to take quick breathers. Indeed, it might seem counterproductive to do so. However, you will only end up doing more when you relax. You can rest for like fifteen minutes after rigorous labour. If you are like me, you can take a nap for twenty minutes and start again. Refreshing yourself will give you the boost to maintain your tenacity for productivity.

**Reframe Your Deadline**

If you are working in an organization, endeavour to seek the permission of your boss early to avoid getting sanctioned. Getting some extra hours or days can be the difference between an average job and a top-quality job. When your boss knows that the delay will increase your efficiency, it is likely he or she give you e more time, which will enable you to work with less stress and pressure. Nonetheless, ensure that you do not have a culture of asking for permission and making excuses.

**Take Advantage of Melody**

Music soothes the soul and can inspire you to keep going when you are feeling like stopping. Have a playlist of inspiring and melodious songs that inspires you. There are always songs that immediately make you feel better and more invigorated. Have them and use them when you need them. Note that music can become a distraction in some cases. So, you need to know when you should play songs or seek other means of motivation. In some situations, you can just play music for a while until you are inspired to focus on the task again.

**Rehydrate**

You will be sluggish when you don't have enough fluid in your body It is always better to rehydrate at the same time you want to take a break so that you will not have reasons to leave the job multiple times. Getting a drink should not become a distraction. So, ensure that you don't let that allow you to get stuck in other activities that can make you lose focus.

## Take One Day for Hard Stuff

Take out a day of the week for doing the most demanding tasks. Of course, you need to plan. List the tasks you need to do that day so that you will not waste time on choosing the activities you need to carry out. Once you do that, the remaining activities of the week will be easier and more interesting. You will do them with less stress, and that bodes well for your mental and physical health.

## Leave Your Comfort Zone

You need to leave your comfort zone to enhance your productivity. For example, being a remote worker does not mean that you have to be working at home in your pyjamas. You may choose to go somewhere you can be more focused on the task if your home is full of potential distractions. For example, if your kids often make you chat more than you should, you need to find somewhere else that ensures that you are engaged. The place might not be as comfortable as your home. However, it is fine as long as it enables you to perform at your best ability.

## Avoid Frowning

The truth is that you will always have reasons to frown and be sad. However, happiness is a choice. You can choose to <u>smile</u> when you may be crying. Indeed, it is easier said than done. However, it is a practice that can boost your mood and help you to avoid procrastination. Your brain knows when you are smiling, and it can improve your entire disposition. If you feel happy, then you will be more willing to get things done, even if you are not truly interested in them.

**Temptation Bundling**

There are things you enjoy doing because they offer you pleasure such as watching your favourite TV show or playing video games. However, there are activities you would prefer not to do even though they are productive such as doing your laundry. You can integrate your temptations into your chores to make them more enjoyable. For example, you can do your laundry while listening to music.

## Eliminate Unproductive Days

Little success here and there will eventually lead to something tangible. You should have a list of the things you need to achieve in a day. Always start immediately to avoid laxity and complacency. Even if you are not able to achieve everything, always ensure that you did some things to pat yourself on the back at the end of the day. If you have a zero-day, you will feel bad about yourself, and that can affect your momentum and motivation the next day.

## Take Advantage of Sprints

When you have unpleasant tasks you need to complete within a short period, the temptation to postpone them is very high. However, you can inspire yourself to get to work by leveraging short sprints. Short sprints are timely frames of blocked time set aside for finishing certain tasks. For example, you can declutter your home in ten minutes by quickly picking unwanted items and disposing of them.

## Chapter Six

## The Final 20 Ways to Overcome Procrastination

It is hard to overcome procrastination, but it is achievable. Of course, there would not have been any need to write this book if it is not achievable. Let us look at the last ways to overcome procrastination.

**The Pomodoro Technique**

This technique has been around since the 1980s. It was created by Francesco Cirillo to help humankind overcome centuries of battling procrastination. The Pomodoro

Technique was created after the popular kitchen timer. It involves ways to work more efficiently to make work more efficient and overcome procrastination. Cirillo realized that human beings cannot focus on two things at the same time. He also understood that people have a limited attention span. So, effectiveness could only be achieved if a person works for a condensed period and take a break before starting again. (9)

The Pomodoro Technique can be broken down into the following steps:

- Select a particular task
- Set a timer for 25 minutes

- Work for 25 minutes without distractions
- Take a five-minute break, which includes getting up and taking a walk
- Resume work for another 25 minutes
- Work for four-time blocks and then take a 15- or 30-minute break

This method aims to challenge your mind to remain focused and fresh by leveraging periodic breaks.

**Leverage your Environment**

You can set up your environment to inspire you to avoid delays. Students often use nudges such as photos and sayings to remind them of their goals. You can do the same thing by filling your surroundings with things that can stir positive emotions. As an adult, you can still inspire yourself by using nudges such as photos, stickers, adages, or other things that can lighten the mood and brighten your day. You can also put your awards to keep reminding you that you have what it takes to succeed again.

## Choose an Overseer

Many people don't want anyone to tell them what to do. However, it is not all bad to have an overseer in your life. An experienced and calm figure who you respect can make a lot of difference. Such a person can help you to ensure that you don't lose focus.

## Embrace Discomfort

Life is not a rollercoaster ride. So, expect things to be tough sometimes. Avoiding discomfort will limit how far you can go. You cannot achieve monumental success if you are willing to pay the price.

**Increase your Work Gradually**

If you do too much at a time, you might be discouraged to start again. Increasing your schedule steadily will enable you to train your body to adjust to new demands without breaking down.

**Evaluate Impact**

Evaluate things based on impact. Does the unpleasant task have a direct impact on your life? If you have answered yes, then decide to commit yourself to complete it promptly. If you need a push, then remember the impact of whatever the consequences of not taking action may be.

## Use Your Strengths

Research has shown that if you use your strengths, then you will increase productivity and improve engagement. We all have strengths that enable us to set goals. So, why not rely on them? (10) When you engage in activities that do not allow you to showcase your capacity, you will look like a fish on dry land.

## Watch Your Diet

One of the worst kept secrets in the world is that what you eat matters. Some food increases your energy and stabilizes your blood sugar. So, if you are feeling sluggish, such food can help you fix the situation.

However, you will need to do some findings to know how to eat them in the right proportion. Note that watching your diet goes beyond simply eating a banana to boost your blood sugar level to complete one task. Rather, it involves checking your feeding habit.

If you don't eat healthy, eating one meal cannot suddenly fix all your problems. You should also find out if you have food allergies by paying attention to the way your body reacts when you consume certain foods. Some people are allergic to gluten. If that is the case for you, you will not be able to work effectively whenever you consume such food.

Some foods can spike up your blood sugar and then drain your energy.

Such foods will impair your performance. They include alcohol, fried foods, fast foods, foods or drinks high in sugar, and refined carbs such as pasta or white bread.

**Don't be too Comfortable**

If care is not taken, comfort can make you too relaxed and procrastinate. When you are working from home, likely, you won't take your bath early in the day and even leave on your pyjamas. However, this approach might prevent you from getting in the mood to work. So, you should consider waking early, taking your bath, and dressing up to be in the mood to start working without wasting time. However, if feeling free enhances your performance, then there is no reason to change.

## Reduce your Expectations

It is good to be ambitious. There is nothing wrong with setting goals and going all out to make them happen. Nonetheless, you should not think that things will always be perfect. A realistic expectation will ensure that you are not so shocked when things don't go your way such that you don't want to do anything again. (10)

## Know When to Give up

You should be resilient. Nonetheless, some situations demand that you give up, and you need to be able to identify them. Don't waste time on something that will not be productive.

## Practice Gratitude

Life will not always give you what you want. So, you need to learn to appreciate your success, regardless of how little it seems. When you do not appreciate what you have, you will be frustrated, and that will affect your effectiveness in your daily activities.

## Be Optimistic

You need to believe the best about your future to keep working hard towards your goals. If you allow negative thoughts drain your energy, it will hamper your performance.

## Be Contented

Contentment does not mean that you should be satisfied with mediocrity. Rather, it is a sense of satisfaction while working hard to achieve more. Lack of contentment will lead to frustration.

## Stay Inspired

You need to stay inspired to keep going and avoid frustration. So, do all you can to keep finding reasons you need to start acting immediately.

## Don't Deceive yourself

Unfortunately, many people put up appearances in the modern world. Many people like to make others see them in a way that is different from who they are in reality. When you are not honest about your progress, you will waste time unnecessarily sometimes.

## Believe in the Process

Everything in life has its time and season. If you are not calm and patient, you will land yourself in trouble. Take time to meditate, relax, and breathe to achieve calmness and encourage your mind to be in the right state for work. (11)

## Don't Overrate yourself

If you don't have an honest evaluation of your ability, you will end up getting stuck along the way, thereby wasting time.

## Don't Hesitate to Ask Questions

Whoever is not too proud to ask questions from the right people is not likely to make mistakes. If such a person has difficulties dealing with an issue, he will be able to find answers to forge ahead on time.

## Be Quick to Repent

You are not impeccable because you are a human being. So, when you make mistakes, you should be quick to admit it. When you don't repent on time, you will inhibit your progress and procrastinate.

Sensei Paul David

## Thank you for reading this book!

If you found this book helpful, I would be grateful if you would post an honest review on Amazon so this book can reach and help other people.

All you need to do is to visit:
**amazon.com/author/senseipauldavid**

click the correct book cover, and finally click on the blue link next to the yellow stars that say, "customer reviews."

***As always… It's a great day to be alive!***

# Check Out Another Book In This Series Visit:

www.amazon.com/author/senseipauldavid

Or

Search Amazon.com #senseipublishing

Sensei Paul David

www.senseipublishing.com

@senseipublishing
#senseipublishing

Check out our **recommendations** for other books for adults & kids plus other great **resources** by visiting

www.senseipublishing.com/resources/

## Join Our Publishing Journey!

If you would like to receive FREE BOOKS and get to know us better, please click www.senseipublishing.com and join our newsletter by entering your email address in the pop-up box.

### Get Our FREE Books Today!
Click & Share the Links Below

### FREE Kids Books
lifeofbailey.senseipublishing.com
kidsonearth.senseipublishing.com

### FREE Self-Development Book
senseiselfdevelopment.senseipublishing.com

Sensei Paul David

## FREE BONUS

## Experience Over 25 FREE Engaging Guided Meditations!

Prized Skills & Practices for Adults & Kids. Help Restore Deep-Sleep, Lower Stress, Improve Posture, Navigate Uncertainty & More.

Download the Free Insight Timer App and click the link below:
**http://insig.ht/sensei_paul**

If you like these meditations & want to go deeper email me for a FREE 30min LIVE Coaching Session:
**senseipauldavid@senseipublishing.com**

## About the Author

I create simple & transformative eBooks & Guided Meditations for Adults & Children proven to help navigate uncertainty, solve niche problems & bring families closer together.

I'm a former finance project manager, private pilot, jiu-jitsu instructor, musician & former University of Toronto Fitness Trainer. I prefer a science-based approach to focus on these & other areas in my life to stay humble & hungry to evolve. I hope you enjoy my work and I'd love to hear your feedback.

It's a great day to be alive!
Sensei Paul David

Sensei Paul David

# Scan & Follow/Like/Subscribe: Facebook, Instagram, YouTube: @senseipublishing

This book is not authorized for free distribution or copying

## Index:

**1.** Genetic Relations Among Procrastination, Impulsivity, and Goal-Management Ability: Implications for the EvolutionaryOriginn of Procrastination

By: Daniel E. Gustavson, Akira Miyake, John K. Hewitt, Naomi P. Friedman

First Published April 4, 2014

Volume: 25 issue: 6, page(s): 1178-1188

Article first published online: April 4, 2014; Issue published: June 1, 2014

https://www.ncbi.nlm.nih.gov/pmc/articles/PMC4185275/

**2.** I forgive myself, now I can study: How self-forgiveness for procrastinating can reduce future procrastination

By Michael J.A.Woh, Timothy A.Pychy, and Shannon H.Bennett of the Carleton University, Department of Psychology,

Article first published online: 26 January 2010, Available online 26 February 2010.

https://www.sciencedirect.com/science/article/pii/S0191886910000474#:~:text=As%20self%2Dforgiveness%20is%20a,encourage%20a%20change%20in%20behavior.

**3.** A Formula for Perfect Productivity: Work for 52 Minutes, Break for 17 Minutes

By Derek Thompson

Article first published online: 17 Septemeber, 2014

https://www.theatlantic.com/business/archive/2014/09/science-tells-you-how-many-minutes-should-you-take-a-break-for-work-17/380369/

4. Solving the Procrastination Puzzle: A Concise Guide to Strategies for Change

By Timothy A. Pychyl

Published 21 December 2013 and available at:

https://www.amazon.com/Solving-Procrastination-Puzzle-Concise-Strategies/dp/0399168125

5. A zeigarnik-like effect in the recall of anagram solutions

By Baddeley, A.

Published: 1 March 1963

https://journals.sagepub.com/doi/abs/10.1080/17470216308416553

6. New study analyzes why people are resistant to correcting misinformation, offers solutions

By Jared Wadley

Article first published online: 20 September 2012

https://news.umich.edu/new-study-analyzes-why-people-are-resistant-to-correcting-misinformation-offers-solutions/

**7.** Students lack interest or motivation

By Carnegie Melon University

Article first published online: 2020

https://www.cmu.edu/teaching/solveproblem/strat-lackmotivation/lackmotivation-01.html

**8.** Learning, Remembering, Believing, Enhancing Human Performance

Consensus Study Report

By Daniel Druckman and Robert A. Bjork,

First published: 1994

https://www.nap.edu/read/2303/chapter/1

9. The Pomodoro Technique: How to Master Your Time in 25-Minute Blocks

By Francesco Cirillo

First published online: 3 August 2020

https://www.developgoodhabits.com/pomodoro-technique/

10. Seven Signs You Are Too Much of a Perfectionist

By Walden University

Published: No recorded publishing date

https://www.waldenu.edu/online-masters-programs/ms-in-psychology/resource/seven-signs-you-are-too-much-of-a-perfectionist

www.ingramcontent.com/pod-product-compliance
Lightning Source LLC
Chambersburg PA
CBHW071715040426
42446CB00011B/2068